MASK MAKING

CHESTER J. ALKEMA

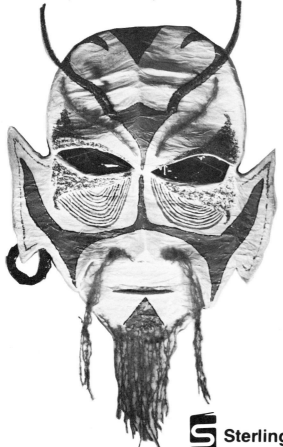

Sterling Publishing Co., Inc.   New York
Distributed in the U.K. by Blandford Press

Library of Congress Cataloging in Publication Data

Alkema, Chester Jay.
  Mask making.

  "A combined edition of Masks, © 1971, and Monster mask, © 1973."
  Includes index.
  Summary: Provides step-by-step instructions for making ghoulish and other kinds of masks from such materials as egg cartons, paper, and plastic foam.
  1. Masks. [1. Masks. 2. Handicraft]
I. Alkema, Chester Jay. Masks.   II. Alkema, Chester Jay. Monster masks.   III. Title.
TT898.A43   731'.75   80-54343
ISBN 0-8069-7038-3
ISBN 0-8069-7039-1 (lib. bdg.) AACR2

ISBN 0-8069-7744-2 (paper)

First paperback printing 1983

"Mask Making"
copyright © 1981 by Sterling Publishing Co., Inc.
Two Park Avenue, New York, N.Y. 10016
is a combined edition of "Masks" © 1971 and
"Monster Masks" © 1973 by Sterling Publishing Co., Inc.
Distributed in Australia by Oak Tree Press Co., Ltd.
P.O. Box K514 Haymarket, Sydney 2000, N.S.W.
Distributed in the United Kingdom by Blandford Press
Link House, West Street, Poole, Dorset BH15 1LL, England
Distributed in Canada by Oak Tree Press Ltd.
℅ Canadian Manda Group, P.O. Box 920, Station U
Toronto, Ontario, Canada M8Z 5P9
Manufactured in the United States of America
All rights reserved

Contents

Before You Begin

As you will see, the masks in this book can be made from a number of materials, including metal. While the simplest and most easily worn masks are made from paper, there are hundreds of possibilities for creating unique masks even with this convenient, safe and inexpensive substance. A plain paper bag placed over your head simply begs for decoration, and shapes you construct from sturdy paper—cylinders, cubes and cones—suggest certain features because of the bumps and flat planes on the surface.

A papier mâché mask requires more preparation than a plain paper mask, but it can be more elaborately decorated. Papier mâché, which dries to an almost rock-hard surface, is very sturdy and will support any heavy embellishments you might want to add—Christmas tree ornaments as ear-rings, marbles as eyes, mirrors to highlight cheek-bones, a flashbulb as a nose, etc. These adornments may be heavy, yet they can also be more fragile than yarn, pipe cleaners or paper would be. After completing an elaborate head, the wall would be the safest place for it.

Early Africans made wood, bone, or ivory masks which they carved into protective spirits, either human or animal, and which they wore at religious ceremonies. On the other side of the world, the American Indian created wooden masks to chase away evil demons, while the Romans and Greeks used masks in the theatre to represent emotions—joy, hate, anger.

So study the pictures to learn the little tricks that will make your masks look professional, then let your imagination run wild!

Paper Bag Masks

A plain brown grocery bag provides an invitingly large surface to decorate. Before you begin designing the face, however, try on the bag by slipping it over your head and allowing it to rest on your shoulders. If you can accurately mark the position of your eyes, mouth and nose, do so; if not, have a friend mark them for you while you wear the bag, so you will be able to see and

Illus. 1

Illus. 2

breathe. Use a crayon or pencil, as the girl in Illus. 1 is doing. Be careful not to puncture the bag and injure yourself as you mark.

Have an idea of the type of expression you want your mask to have before you cut any holes in the bag. A surprised face requires large, round eyes, a sad face calls for eyes which slant down at the outer corners, while evil eyes should slant up.

Illus. 3

mask by drawing decorative eyes where you want them to appear, with crayon, pencil or paint.

When the mask in Illus. 3 was designed, its maker realized the limitations of paper—that it cannot support too many heavy ornaments. He took advantage of the smooth nature of the paper and decorated the mask with tempera paint instead of elaborate bangles. The geometric areas of color echo the shapes which he cut away, around both the eyes and mouth. Thin black lines surrounding the differently colored triangles and zig-zags accent these shapes even more.

The paper bag is certainly strong enough to support a pair of cardboard or tagboard ears. The bright colors which appear on the face are repeated in the oddly shaped ears, and make this mask the spectacle that it is. Brass paper fasteners hold these ears to the side of the bag, but glue, staples or tape would attach them just as securely.

If you cut away the side portions around the bottom of the bag, the mask will fit down better over your shoulders and stay on your head securely. The long drooping points which remain and are being painted in Illus. 3 can then become any one of a number of things. Depending on the color they are painted, they might represent the shirt which the monster mask is wearing. Or, they could be the long ends of an elegant moustache. The areas left in back become hair.

The mask in Illus. 2 will probably have evil eyes. If the bag is very tall and the eyes of the mask need to be higher than your own for a realistic face, cut small holes to see through. Then decorate the

Paper Cylinder Masks

When rolled into a cylinder, paper makes an excellent base on which you can design a colorful mask. To make a mask like the one in Illus. 4, roll a sheet of thin manila tagboard and glue the ends together. Cover the tagboard with colored paper and cut shapes of contrasting colors for features. The triangles make this mask look like an Indian decorated with warpaint.

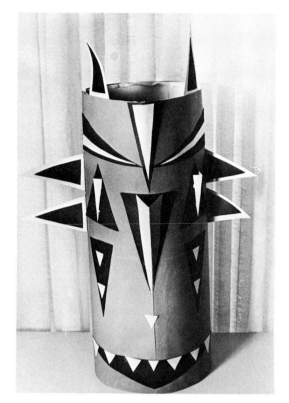

Illus. 4

Illus. 5

The mask in Illus. 5 is very realistic. The features are made of unusual paper shapes, the pupils of the eyes are rolled pipe cleaners, and the hair is yarn. Another substitute for hair is excelsior, the strawlike material used for protection in packaging. Because of its tendency to fly away, excelsior must be firmly glued to the cylinder.

See page 30 for a paper cylinder mask in color.

Paper Totem Pole Masks

Make an extra tall cylinder by taping two ordinary-sized cylinders together. Use two large sheets of tagboard, each one 24″ × 36″, as a base for your totem pole mask. The one in Illus. 6 is composed of three different faces. Some features are painted and others are cut from construction paper. To add even more height to the totem pole, the top head has been made king by being crowned. Paper strips, cut to jagged lengths, are used to imitate eyelashes and a beard. Small paper cylinders form the protruding noses and the top and bottom pair of ears, while the ears in the middle are from flat paper stapled to the tagboard and folded to stick out.

Illus. 6

Paper Cube Masks

Fold a sheet of paper in three places to make a paper cube. The corners provide the bumps which represent the ears and nose of the face. The nose stands away from your face when you wear the mask, so you will be able to breathe easily.

The paper cube mask in Illus. 7 has a striking geometric pattern. The background of the face is blue construction paper, pasted on the tagboard before it is folded. Thin paper strings point to the middle of the mask and echo the 3-dimensional shape of the cube. The strips divide the mask into distinct areas, so the elaborate ears, nose and cheeks stand out.

The eyes of the mask also point to the middle, as do the ears and folded papers on the cheekbones. Even the curled strips above the ears—which might represent hair to the imaginative designer—

Illus. 7

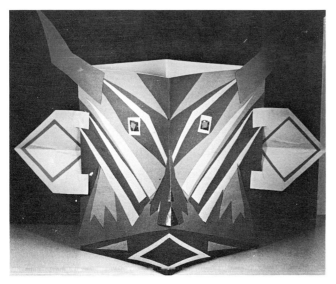

aim toward the nose. The mask does not really look like any animal you have ever seen, but in mask-making, that does not really matter.

Illus. 8. This creature resembles a real animal, due to the colors that are used. The designer copied a tiger when he decorated this mask, and used shades of brown and yellow. Try black and white for a zebra, or gold for a lion.

9

Paper Cone Masks

Make a paper cone to form a sharp nose or jutting chin. Cones are one of the fastest ways of turning flat paper into a base which has shape. Cut a slit or a V-shape in a piece of paper, as in Illus. 9. The larger the area you cut away, the more pointed will be the cone. Attach the sides of the V together with staples, glue or tape on the inside of the cone, and decorate the mask with paint, paper, ornaments and trims. See Illus. 35 and 37 for two paper cone masks in color.

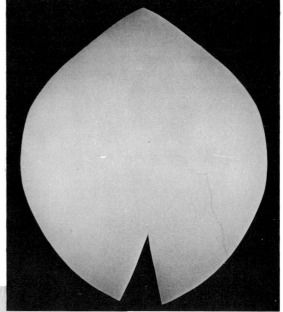

Illus. 9

Illus. 10. Contrasting colors form swirling areas and flowing patterns to make a fearsome dragon face. Illus. 37 shows a tagboard mask in color.

Paper Bas-Relief Masks

Bas-relief is a term used in sculpture and carving to indicate a raised design on a flat surface. You can use this craft technique on your mask to create the features of a face. Cut strips of paper and bend, loop or curl them to any shape (see Illus. 11). To attach the strips to the basic shape of your mask, use either waterproof glue or transparent tape.

Illus. 11

Illus. 12 (left). Something is not pleasing this fellow, as you can see from his scowl. His eyebrows slant down as if he were frowning, and the corners of his mouth turn under, showing how angry he is.

Illus. 13 (right). It's not hard to make a cheery face: use light colors, and compose the features so they point upward. To wear these masks, insert brass paper fasteners on each side just above the ears. Tie string to the fasteners and slip the mask over your head. See Illus. 38 for a bas-relief mask in color.

11

Paper Monofold Masks

One of the easiest masks to make is a monofold mask, a sheet of construction paper folded in half lengthwise and cut and decorated with various shapes. The monofold mask is similar to the paper cube (see page 9), but here there is no back to the mask.

Illus. 14

Fold the construction paper in half and lightly outline the areas you will cut away. Then use a pair of sharp scissors to cut. Because the paper is folded in half, the two sides will be symmetrical. Decorate the folded mask with paint, paper strips, aluminum foil, as in Illus. 15, or simply with paper shapes in contrasting colors, as in Illus. 14. For a monofold mask in color, see Illus. 66.

Illus. 15

Paper Plate Masks

An ordinary paper plate provides an excellent base upon which you can design unusual faces. The round plate is the proper shape for a face, and it is sturdy enough to support attached ornaments. To transform a plain paper plate into a festive face like the one in Illus. 16, draw on the plate with soft-tip marking pens in assorted colors. The markers are easy to use, but you might prefer crayons or tempera paint instead.

The pieces surrounding the face are parts of other paper plates; they represent ears, a beard and a crown. These spokes radiating from the original plate make the mask look like the face of a king, while the lines on the rippled border also carry the eye further away from the plate itself, toward the spokes. Learn to use the background texture of your materials to your advantage, to make your mask a unified creation rather than a random assortment of materials.

Illus. 16

Paper Collage Masks

A popular art form today is "collage," the pasting together of many different pieces of paper, newspaper, or other objects to form a bizarre arrangement of items not usually associated with one another. Just look at the example here to see how weird a mask with a collage in the background can be! The eyes seem to be peering out from a head befuddled with noise, confusion and important issues—all representative of our modern world. The smile is so artificial that it must be labelled "smile." The confusion and artificiality of the mask is purposeful: it expresses the feelings of the mask-maker regarding the constant bombardment of his senses in these frantically active times.

Look through several magazines and newspapers and choose pictures and headlines which appeal to you. Cover a tagboard cylinder with the cut-outs, and paint features on the mask with tempera paint or crayon.

The mask in color in Illus. 67 is a paper collage mask. The base is a paper cone covered with newspaper clippings, and the features are made of construction paper accented with tempera paint. The hair is curled wire.

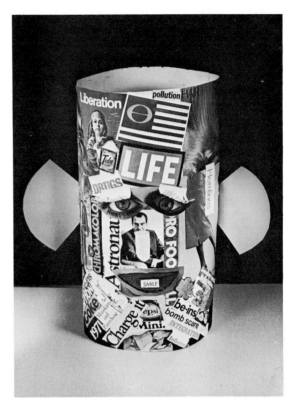

Illus. 17

14

Construction Paper Masks

What can you do with construction paper? You can cut it, fold, curl, and bend it, paint and draw on it, and attach other papers and trims to its surface. To make the outline of a construction paper mask, hold a piece of large construction paper up to your face. Have a friend outline an area 2″ above your hairline, down the sides of your face, and well below your chin in a general shape which you will later alter. Ask your friend to mark places on the sides above each ear for sidebands that will rest on the top of your ears when you wear the mask.

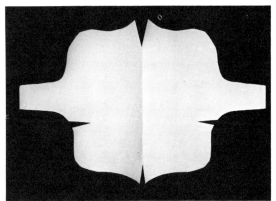

Illus. 18

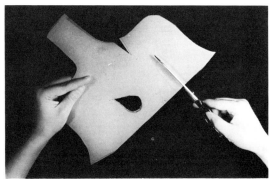

Illus. 19

Correct the outline of the mask, cutting slits for cone shapes if you want the mask to jut out. (See Illus. 18 for a completed mask pattern.) Mark the position of the eyes, nose and mouth. Cut out these areas in unusual shapes, as in Illus. 19, and staple or glue the sides of the slits together. The mask in Illus. 20 is almost completed; see the finished mask in Illus. 43. Another construction paper mask appears in Illus. 36.

Illus. 20

15

Illus. 21. Different colored construction paper shapes make this fierce warrior mask a terrifying sight. The beard is made of black construction paper which was slit and curled.

Illus. 22. This clever face was designed as a wall hanging and is not meant to be worn. The face is oval and was pasted to a dark background. The glasses, cigar, bow tie and heavy moustache and eyebrows tell you at once who this mask represents: Groucho.

PAPIER MÂCHÉ MASKS

Objects made from papier mâché at least 2,000 years ago have been discovered. This craft material is not a new one, then, but it certainly is long-lasting. Its durability makes it ideal for use in decorative (not wearable) masks. The materials necessary for papier mâché are always available, and the finished object, once it has dried to a hard, smooth surface, makes an inviting area to decorate. In making masks of papier mâché, you usually shape the wet newspaper over a form, to give it the proper shape. The specific form you are working with determines exactly how you should shape and manipulate the papier mâché.

Papier Mâché over a Bowl

This method of forming a hard mask is not the usual papier mâché technique, as you do not tear the paper into strips. Instead, you will paste four layers of newspaper half-sheets together and mould the shape over a bowl. The mask in Illus. 55 was made this way. After the paper was hard and dry, the mask-maker cut and glued strips of colored tissue paper to the edges of the mask.

Assemble all your materials before you begin. You will need four half-sheets or tabloid-size sheets of preferably clean white newspaper, library or flour paste the consistency of light cream, a shallow glass bowl and a pair of scissors. Since you cannot decorate the mask until it is completely dry, you do not need to gather your paints and ornaments yet.

Use a small paint brush or the brush that comes in the jar of library paste to cover one side of one sheet of newspaper. Place another sheet on top of the first. Continue until you have pasted all four sheets together, as in Illus. 23.

Illus. 23

17

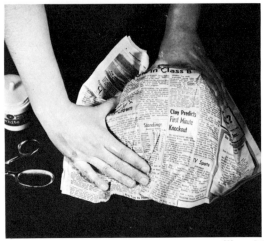

Illus. 24

Illus. 25

Before the paste dries, mould the four pasted (laminated) sheets over the bowl, curving the paper to conform to the bowl's curves. While the paper is still damp, trim the edges evenly around the rim with the scissors. You may want to leave part of the excess newspaper to represent horns, ears or a beard.

Set aside the glass bowl with the damp paper on it to dry at least overnight. Then lift the hardened paper off the bowl, and decorate it with paint, paper or heavier ornaments. If you use printed newspaper it will be more difficult to cover with paint.

You should not wear this mask as you will not be able to breathe or see, but because it is sturdy, you can decorate it with many objects to make an unusual wall hanging.

Papier Mâché: Strip Method

The strip method of papier mâché allows you to form more detailed features on your mask. The newspaper is not put on in one sheet but rather in narrow strips, one at a time. By building up the layers of the mask slowly, and by squeezing excess moisture and any air bubbles out of the layers as you progress, you will construct a mask that is smooth, sturdy and ready to decorate.

Assemble these materials: newspaper as before, library paste or flour paste which is the consistency of light cream, and a base. (See the following projects which use a variety of bases to determine which one you want to use.) Tear the sheets of newspaper lengthwise (with the "grain") into strips about 1″ wide. You can tell the grain direction by a simple test—it is the direction in which the paper tears more easily. Make some strips narrower than 1″, to form the details of the face after the basic head is dry.

Using a large, shallow pan (an aluminum baking dish or roasting pan is practical; the paste rinses out with soap and water), pour about half an inch of paste on the bottom. Soak the newspaper strips in the paste until they are saturated with the mixture, and begin to cover the base.

Lift one strip at a time from the pan and place it smoothly on the base. Smooth the pasted strip with your fingers from the middle to the ends, to eliminate any air bubbles or lumps of paste. Cover the base with one layer of strips horizontally, and then place a second layer at right angles to the first. Place the third and fourth layers diagonally on top of the others. Alternating the direction of the newspaper strips guarantees complete, even coverage of the base, and smoothing each strip as you apply it helps build a hard mask.

Before you allow the paste to dry, trim the edges of the mask with a scissors as you did when you used newspaper sheets over a bowl (page 18). Then set aside the mask for a day or so, preferably in sunlight, to let all the moisture evaporate. For quick drying you can bake it at a low heat in the oven. When the mask is hard and dry, decorate it with paints, paper and other ornaments. Use facial tissue dipped in paste to build up small areas, such as a nose, the ridge of the eyebrow, or a chin.

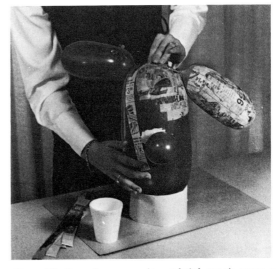

Illus. 26. Forming a papier mâché mask over a balloon base.

Papier Mâché over Balloons

Balloons are just the right size and shape for covering with papier mâché. Although you cannot wear the masks you form over balloons, because there are no openings to breathe through, the round shape will contribute to a realistic face. Cover the front half of a large balloon with newspaper strips, and when they have hardened, burst the balloon and pull it away from the papier mâché shell. Trim the edges of the mask with a pair of sturdy scissors so it is smooth and even. Then decorate the face with paint and other items.

The balloon base which is being covered with newspaper strips in Illus. 26 is really made of four balloons: a large one forms the head, while two medium ones are attached with masking tape to the central balloon for ears, and a small round balloon is taped for a nose. After all the layers of newspaper have been put on the balloons, it will be impossible to tell that where there is now one surface there were once four balloons! It doesn't matter if the air goes out or the balloons burst, once your layers have dried.

To help you while you attach the papier mâché strips, support the balloon on a circular band cut from tagboard (see Illus. 26). You might want to

Illus. 27. Colored tissue paper instead of newspaper is the fourth layer of this papier mâché mask. Wool yarn and glitter define the unusual shapes, and a tightly rolled sheet of newspaper curves around the head for horns. Toothpick boxes, covered with glitter, contain jacks and dangle as earrings.

Illus. 28. This gigantic papier mâché mask, formed over a large balloon, becomes even bigger when decorated. Paper plates are attached to both sides and then painted to serve as ears; round mirrors glued to drinking cups form protruding eyes; a strand of Christmas tinsel makes an elegant nose-ring; and newspaper tubes covered with papier mâché become eyebrows and tusks. The entire head is enlivened by tempera paints. To see a papier mâché mask formed over a balloon in color, turn to Illus. 49.

layer this band with newspaper also, to give the mask a permanent base upon which it can stand later, after the central balloon has burst. Remember to trim the excess newspaper around the edge of the band before the paste has hardened.

Papier Mâché over Crushed Newspaper

Sheets of newspaper that have been tightly crushed into an oval shape (or a more unusual shape, if you want) provide a sturdy base on which to build a papier mâché mask. Use as many sheets as necessary to make a sufficiently large base, and tie the base tightly with string to keep it together. Tape the crushed newspaper base to a table top and lay a water-soaked sheet of newspaper over the base. Tape this also to the table. The wet sheet will make it easy later when you remove the mask shell from the crushed newspaper base.

Using the method described on page 19, layer newspaper strips saturated with paste over the top and sides of the wet sheet of newspaper. While the mask is drying, assemble the materials you will use to decorate the face. Masks formed over crushed newspaper, like the ones in Illus. 48, 59 and 62, can be decorated with any articles you have on hand. The masks in color use yarn, glitter, soft-tip pens, tempera paint and twine to form their bizarre faces. You can improvise with almost any trinket to form some facial feature.

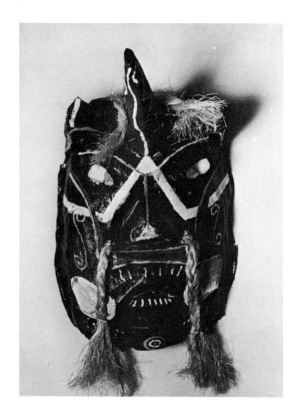

Illus. 29. Paper towels soaked in paste are the last layer here, to give this monster a baby-soft complexion. Binding twine makes the moustache and hair. The entire surface of the face is covered with black tempera paint and then shellac, for a shiny surface.

Papier Mâché over Clay

Modelling clay is an excellent base over which to form papier mâché masks. As you can model the base with any details you want, the finished face also appears just like a real face rather than only a smooth surface decorated with baubles. Remember, however, that the features in clay should be very exaggerated, because the layers of newspaper strips that you add will tend to level out any small hollows and bumps. To make sure that the area around the nose and eye sockets is hollow on your finished mask, make these parts very deep on the clay base. The pictures on the next page demonstrate how the papier mâché evens the surface slightly.

After you have modelled the clay face the way you want it, apply petroleum jelly liberally over the surface of the clay, making sure that it gets on to all parts of the face. Removing the clay from the dried papier mâché is much easier if you take this simple step. Then you can model the clay again for another mask.

Illus. 30

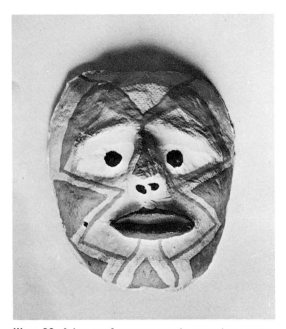

Illus. 31. A close view of a clay base. Notice the exaggerated features: deep hollows below the cheekbones, protruding lips, large eye sockets. Clay is a wonderful modelling material and can be built into any shape. Because you can re-use it later, it is economical as well.

Illus. 32. A layer of paper towels, torn into strips and soaked in paste, gives the surface of this mask an unusual texture. While the features of the face are 3-dimensional, not merely painted, they are not as distinct as those on the clay model. See Illus. 60 for a color view.

Papier Mâché over Aluminum Foil

Two thicknesses of aluminum foil make a sturdy base over which you can easily apply papier mâché. An outstanding advantage of using foil as a base is that you can mould it on your own face, or have a friend do it for you (see Illus. 33),

and thus duplicate your own facial features. While the foil is on your face, keep your eyes closed. Try to mould the foil as quickly as possible so you are not cut off from your air supply for too long. Trim the excess around the face so that it does not extend beyond the hairline, ears or chin. If you do not do this, you will have a frame of excess papier mâché around the face.

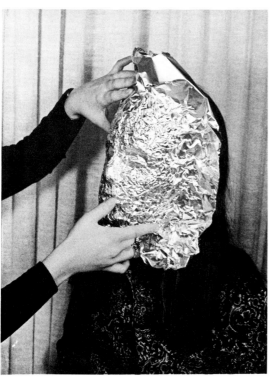

Illus. 33

Illus. 34. Even though this mask was formed over a foil base, chances are the model for the base would never recognize herself! Op art designs and swirls radiate around the middle, and wire sculpture earrings continue the circular pattern.

Illus. 35. A large tagboard cone forms the central part of this paper mask covered with foil.

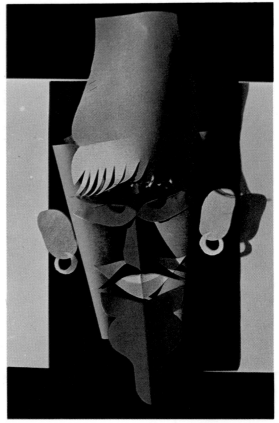

Illus. 36. Construction paper is easily bent and folded to create a 3-dimensional shape. All parts of this mask are made of construction paper. This would make a dramatic wall hanging.

26

Illus. 37. This easily constructed tagboard mask is decorated with tempera paints.

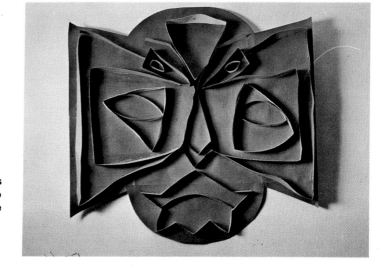

Illus. 38. Contruction paper strips of different colors are glued on to the basic shape to form the features.

Illus. 39. Mounted on stiff construction paper, this mask built over an aluminum foil mould has a crown of yarn to decorate the head.

Illus. 40. Bold colors, wide eyes, evil ears and long fangs contribute to the awful appearance of this monster's head, formed over a foil base.

Papier Mâché
over Chipboard

Chipboard, or thick cardboard, comes in many different weights, and depending on the thickness, should be sawed with a jig saw or cut with a razor blade or scissors. If you are not experienced with a saw, get someone to help you who is. The chipboard base requires some careful advance preparation before you can begin to layer newspaper strips on it, but the trouble you go to now is well worth it. The unusual curves and bumps which appear on the finished mask, planned by you at the start, cannot be duplicated by using any other base.

Before you or your helper begin cutting the basic outline of your mask, sketch it with a light pencil on the chipboard, so you have a guide to follow as you cut. Don't try to get too fancy: avoid elaborate curves or extremely narrow sections such as horns and ears. Not only are these difficult to cut from thick chipboard, but they might snap off either as you work with the base or later, on the finished papier mâché mask.

To make some parts of the face stand out more than others, such as the nose, eyebrows, chin and cheekbones, glue separate layers of chipboard on top of each other. Start with a piece of chipboard that covers the entire area of the particular feature, and on each layer glue a piece slightly smaller.

Illus. 41. If you saw the chipboard for the base of your mask, do it very carefully. Be sure your saw is sharp enough to cut without difficulty.

Illus. 42. Any kind of paper can be rolled into a cylinder to form a mask that fits over your head.

Illus. 43. To make a face mask that will fit you exactly, hold the paper over your face and have someone sketch the positions of your features. Then decorate according to your whim.

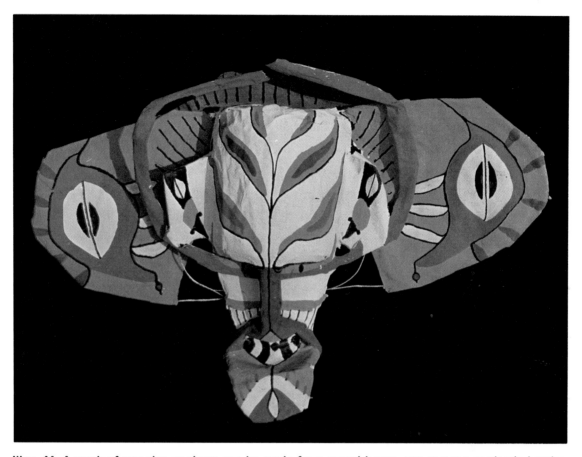

Illus. 44. A mask of any size or shape can be made from cereal boxes, egg cartons or plastic bottles, joined together with masking tape and covered with a special paper such as tissue. This unusual mask has a plastic bottle body. Wire loops form the ears and the entire mask is covered with papier mâché.

To see how these layers are built up piece by piece, look at Illus. 45. The areas for the eyes and fangs which will later be painted on the final layer of papier mâché are already sketched in, to guide the mask-maker when he glues the small pieces of chipboard to the face. A small piece of rolled cardboard, glued to the middle of the forehead perpendicular to the face, will become a horn. While you will be able to make slight changes in the mask's surface as you apply the papier mâché by using extra strips of newspaper or tissue, the major portion of the shaping depends on the base itself.

The partially completed mask in Illus. 46 has newspaper strips covering its surface to round off the angles which were formed by the different layers of chipboard. Every part of the face has the same number of newspaper strips, but the difference in the height and depth of the surface is levelled somewhat by the newspaper which joins the various areas. The finished mask is in color in Illus. 51.

Illus. 45

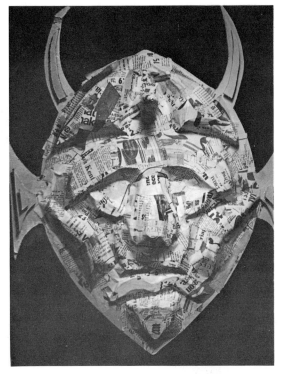

Illus. 46

Papier Mâché over Container Base

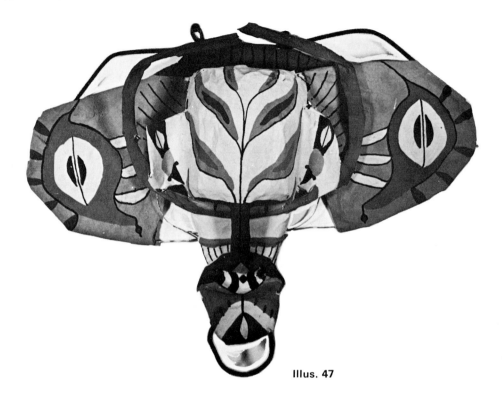

Illus. 47

Instead of moulding or sawing a base for your papier mâché mask, make use of the many shapes and sizes of containers which are available. Some cartons or bottles are just the right size to build a mask around, while others are perfect for a particular feature: a bathroom tissue tube for a nose, or egg carton sections for eyes. Using a disposable container for a base not only saves you the time it would take to build a base, but helps cut down on pollution by making practical use of what would otherwise be another piece of waste. The mask in Illus. 47 (shown in color on page 31) has as its base a plastic bottle which once contained starch. The bottle's handle becomes the nose, and wire loops poked into the bottle and covered with papier mâché are the ears.

33

Illus. 48 (right). Newspapers crushed into a football shape provide the foundation of this papier mâché mask. Glitter and a soft-tip pen were used on the face, and black yarn hair completed the fearsome mask.

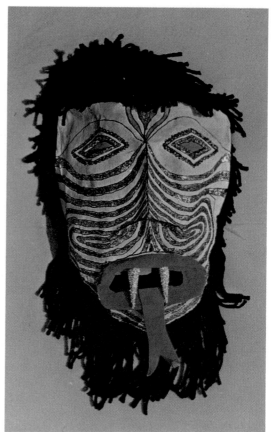

Illus. 49 (left). A balloon forms the base of this papier mâché mask. Paper drinking cups serve as eyes. Plastic foam balls make up the cheeks and eyeballs. Construction paper, yarn, pipe cleaners, aluminum foil and tempera paints add the finishing touches.

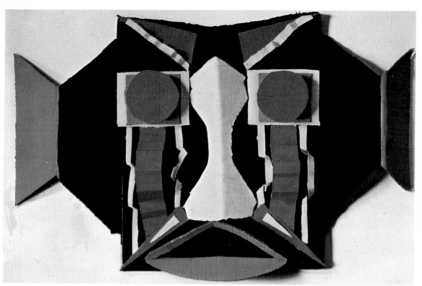

Illus. 50 (above). Corrugated cardboard strips and pieces add dimension as well as decoration to the basic paper shape.

Illus. 51 (left). Chipboard serves as a base for this papier mâché mask, which has been painted with tempera.

Papier Mâché over Cardboard

A flat shape cut from corrugated cardboard makes a sturdy base if you want only slightly raised facial features. The mask in color in Illus. 65 looks evil because of the large flat cheeks and forehead. Facial tissues soaked in paste form the nose and eyebrow regions. This raises them just enough to differentiate the sections of the face, but not enough to detract from the colorful painted features. The final layer of papier mâché, on both the mask in color and the one on this page, is tissue paper rather than newspaper.

In the mask in Illus. 52, small rolls of newspaper lie right under the surface of the tissue paper layer. The rolls, made from only a small piece of paper, create many variations on the surface of this face: the lips, for example, are more prominent because of the small amount of height they gain from the rolls. After being painted, they are even more grotesque, a feature you might strive for when you design your own monsters.

Illus. 52. Marbles, embedded in the papier mâché before it dries, make sparkling eyes. Beads hang from the corners of the mouth, and a shiny tongue—metallic paper over wire—adds to this mask's appeal.

Two-Dimensional Faces

Double-walled corrugated cardboard from grocery cartons is sturdy enough to support many different objects, so you can cut a simple square face and then decorate it freely with all sorts of unusual things. The cardboard is light enough to wear, if you cut eyeholes and air vents in the face. Attach string or elastic to both sides of the cardboard with brass paper fasteners and tie the mask on your head, to present your friends with a new you!

The mask in Illus. 53 (and another in color in Illus. 61) shows what elaborate lengths you can go to when you decorate a flat cardboard face. If you want to make a mask similar to the one here, follow these directions. First, cut out the eyeholes, making sure that they are positioned correctly not only as you look at the mask, but also as you look though it. The point of having eyeholes is for you to be able to see, so be sure you can see through before you wear the mask. Using rubber cement or another all-purpose yet strong glue, attach an unusual nose: a carrot (with or without the carrot greens), a raw beet, a banana or, as in the mask here, a gourd. Of course, you could even use a paper cone, but because the cardboard face is so plain, you should add the most outlandish ornaments you can find.

Only on a bizarre mask like this could you find cornhusk ears and notebook binder rings through the nose. The mouth is made of nails and bobby pins, while twine hair, cornhusks and feathers decorate the top of the cardboard. There is even some jewelry: beads hang as a hair ornament and door keys become earrings. Try your hand at making the weirdest mask you can, using trinkets from every part of the house.

Illus. 53

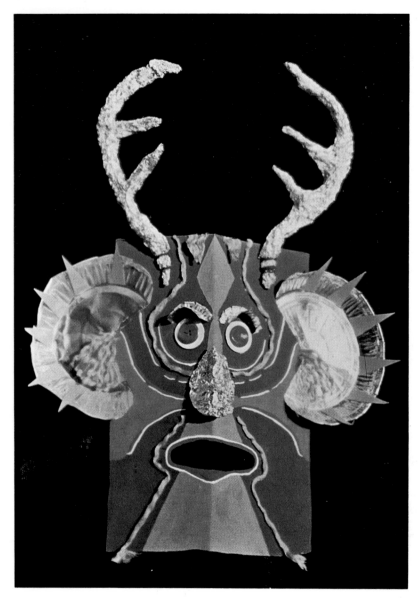

Illus. 54. Make a single vertical fold in a piece of cardboard, add pie plate ears, aluminum foil horns, yarn and buttons, and you have a fantastic monster mask!

Illus. 55. Four layers of paper laid over a shallow glass bowl create this colorful papier mâché mask.

Cardboard Bas-Relief Masks

Corrugated cardboard makes sturdy 3-dimensional masks as well as flat faces; the cardboard bends in one direction, at its ridges. It folds around itself, and is thick enough to stack for extra height. The hands in Illus. 56 are glueing the edges of the triangular mouth to the flat cardboard base. To make the mouth stand out even more (as it is in Illus. 57), glue only the bottom corners. For a nose that rises above the rest of the face, fold your shape in half vertically. The maker of this mask cut four slits in the cardboard backing, through which she inserted the four corners of the nose. Glue might not have held the nose as securely as the slits do.

The eyes and eyebrows are unusual parts of this mask. Peel a piece of corrugated cardboard apart and notice the different layers. One of these inner layers, attached loosely above the eyes, makes wavy eyebrows. The eyes themselves pop out here because the circular portion—the eyeball—is glued on top of a rectangle of corrugated cardboard. To make such a rectangle, fold a strip of cardboard in the same direction in three places, glue the edges together, and attach one flat side to the cardboard face.

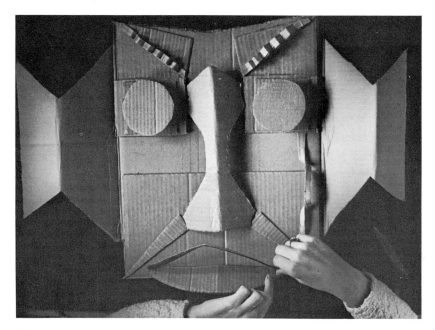

Illus. 56. Cardboard is sturdy enough for the base, yet flexible enough to form the face.

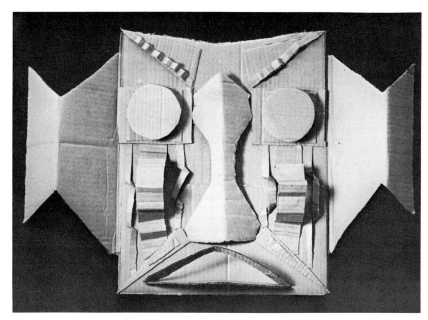

Illus. 57. Wavy cheek sections protrude like the letter C. To see the finished mask in color, turn to Illus. 50.

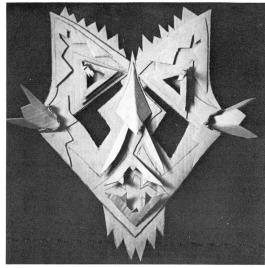

Illus. 58. To contribute to an even greater 3-dimensional effect, cut out parts of the base, leave some areas flat, and stack layers on other sections.

Illus. 59. Tempera paints and binding twine decorate the surfaces of this papier mâché mask, which was constructed over crushed paper.

Illus. 60. This papier mâché mask was built over a clay base.

Illus. 61 (right). Ribbed black corrugated cardboard is the background for a whimsical African mask. Scouring pads and pipe cleaners adorn the warrior.

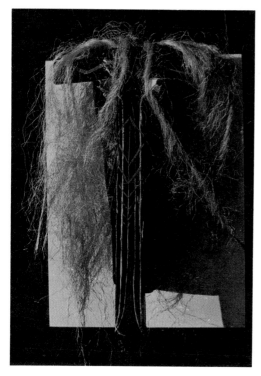

Illus. 62 (left). A long piece of plastic foam makes a bizarre nose while egg carton sections form protruding eyes of a papier mâché mask made over crushed paper.

43

Cardboard Monofold Masks

Do you remember making monofold masks from paper? See page 12 if you need to refresh your memory. Making monofold masks in cardboard is basically the same as in paper: fold a flat sheet of corrugated cardboard vertically down the middle, so that it stands away from your face when you wear it, and decorate the face in any fanciful way you please. Attach brass paper fasteners and string or elastic on both sides of the mask above the ears to keep the mask on your head when you wear it. The mask in color on page 38 and the one here are both cardboard monofold masks. Although the mask in Illus. 63 has no eyeholes, it makes a vibrant decoration on a wall.

Illus. 63. Aluminum pie pans highlight the eyes, made of buttons and underlined with dark tempera paint. The geometric areas on the face, formed by the different colored paints, point toward the tissue paper mouth.

Cardboard Carton Masks

Cardboard cartons or small boxes make excellent foundations upon which you can design a monster face. A shoe box, with the bottom portion cut away to form the chin, is the base of this mask. Foil and tinsel combine to make this mask twinkle and shine above all the others. Fragments of a Christmas tree decoration perch at the top of this mask to imitate sparkling hair. Aluminum pie pans give a startled, wide-awake look to our friend, and flashbulbs, as used on camera flash attachments, add an extra bit of brilliance to his appearance. Tempera paint fills in the few areas that are not 3-dimensional.

Masks can be plain or elaborate, made of paper, cardboard, or sturdy papier mâché, built upon almost any base, and decorated with just about any material available in any type of store. You have seen a parade of unusual faces in the examples given here—begin now to design your own gallery of monsters!

Illus. 64

Illus. 65. A flat shape cut from corrugated cardboard with a papier mâché tissue paper covering has an eerie look when painted and decorated.

Illus. 66. A monofold mask is made by cutting a piece of folded construction paper into this interesting shape.

Illus. 67. Paper collage masks are fun to make. Tear and cut pictures and patterns from magazines to decorate your masks. This one is made on a shallow construction paper cone.

Seed and Gravel Masks

Seeds and aquarium gravel provide an abundance of colored material for use in your mask-making.

Aquarium gravel comes in a great range of colors, although the size and shape is more or less uniform. However, seeds offer a variety of color, size and texture. For those seeds and

Illus. 69. If you want to know how this rare rabbit turned out, see color Illus. 102.

Illus. 68. This sinister mask is made of sunflower seeds, dyed cantaloupe and pumpkin seeds, and squash seeds, all glued onto a piece of white flannel.

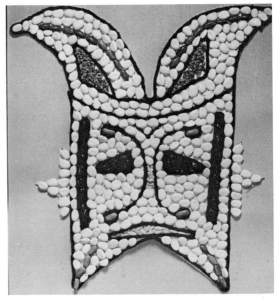

Illus. 70. Lima beans, green beans, beet seeds, celosia seeds, wax-bean seeds and cucumber seeds mix well together on the surface, but may possibly have caused a severe case of indigestion judging from his sullen expression.

Illus. 71. This is certainly not that merry old soul, King Cole! His Highness is composed of an unsettling grouping of lima-bean, beet, radish, and cucumber seeds glued on painted tagboard.

Illus. 72. Colored aquarium gravel hardened the fixed expression on this monstrous mask. The soft-tip-pen contours of the design were left exposed to add emphasis to the variously colored areas.

grains that are neutral, such as rice and certain types of corn, you can use food coloring to dye them. Watermelon seeds, sunflower seeds, red Indian corn, kidney beans, split dried peas, barley, oats, bright yellow field corn are among the colorful seeds that will help you create delightful monster masks.

Just look at the range of effects in the illustrations. Each kind of seed was chosen carefully to heighten the effects of the all-over designs. Elongated seeds are appropriate for the long smirking mask in Illus. 68, while round puffy seeds emphasize the pouting monarch in Illus. 70.

49

Crayoned Masks

You can use the simple crayon in a variety of ways to produce different and exciting effects. There have been so many new kinds of crayons developed in recent years that you can be deceived into thinking certain results could never have been crayoned. In addition, there are many techniques that you can try in your mask-making—crayon resist, crayon etching, stencils, crayon relief, melted crayons, and so on.

The unsettling looking face in Illus. 74 was

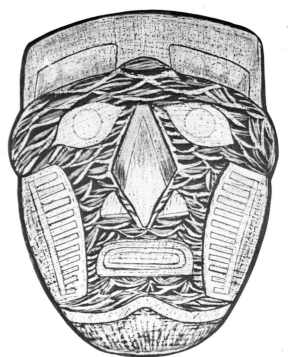

Illus. 74. Blue, red and yellow crayon with a black tempera wash created this morbid crayon-resist ghoul.

Illus. 73. A crayon cut-throat, drawn and colored on tagboard. Punch holes in his ears with brass paper fasteners to hold an elastic band, and they'll double as earrings.

given life by the crayon-resist technique on manila paper. Here, you apply crayon heavily in such a way that you leave many small areas uncolored. Then lay on a wash of black tempera paint over the entire design. The wash will resist the crayoned areas and permeate the uncolored areas of the paper, creating a brilliant, intense effect. Depending upon the kind of mask you are making, you can experiment with dark washes over light colors, light washes over dark colors, using

Illus. 75.

Illus. 76.

Illus. 77.

either light or dark paper. Or, your monster might require several coats of wash to give exactly the right impression. Instead of manila paper, try construction paper or tagboard. The slight speckling or flecked appearance created by the crayon-resist technique adds a nice touch of unreality.

Take your pick of the fiendish charmers in Illus. 75, 76 and 77. Here you can see how the same design can be altered drastically by the technique you use. So if your mood dictates a somewhat less ferocious mask, you can use plain crayons on tagboard such as in Illus. 75, leaving narrow uncrayoned borders between each color area. This will allow for the change of mood in Illus. 76, where the same mask has

been subjected to a crayon-etching treatment, resulting in a more alarming-looking demon.

Since you are going to apply a wash of black India ink over the entire surface of the mask, make a tissue paper tracing of your design first and label the shapes and colors so you'll remember where they all are. After applying the ink and allowing it to dry thoroughly, using a scissors point or other sharp instrument, scratch off the ink. Notice that the scratching in Illus. 76 was all done in a vertical direction. The borders that you leave uncovered will retain the ink. If you wish, you can substitute crayon for the India ink and manila paper for the tagboard. However, tagboard is smoother and thicker

51

and the etching tool is less likely to scratch the surface.

Crayon combined with painted lines produced the hostile fellow in Illus. 77. Borders and spots were left uncrayoned round color areas and were then painted in with an Oriental bamboo brush dipped in India ink.

The gruesome beast in Illus. 78 proves the theory of "Waste Not, Want Not." Scrap crayons, all those little butts and stumps that are usually thrown away, can be put to good use in your mask-making. Painting with melted wax is an ancient practice and creates stunning effects. You can melt your wax crayons in an electric palette made just for

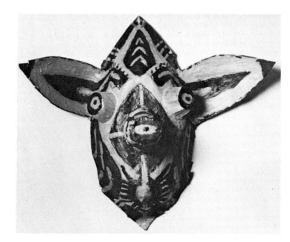

Illus. 79. Who would believe this gruesome creature's evil eyes are nothing more than innocuous little paper cups!

that purpose (Illus. 78), or place crayons of the same colors in small juice cans and set them in a pan of boiling water until melted. Then, while you are working, place the cans in an electric frying pan turned to a low temperature.

The completed monster in Illus. 79 was painted in black and red with a $\frac{1}{2}$-inch-wide bristle brush on a papier mâché mask which was constructed over a bowl. This method requires pasting four layers of newspaper together and moulding them over a bowl. Set the bowl with the paste-soaked paper aside to dry overnight. When completely hard, you can start decorating it. Don't attempt to wear this kind of mask—it's strictly for decoration.

Illus. 78. Here, a papier mâché mask is being painted with melted crayons.

Painted Masks

Tempera paint can be used in a variety of exciting ways to create a mask monster. Although many clowns are sad, few are menacing as is the one in Illus. 80. This is one clown that would never make the circus— he would scare everyone away! His creator, in Illus. 81, first drew the design on tagboard with a ballpoint pen and then cut it out and painted it with tempera in bold swirling colors.

A very satisfying ghoul can be rendered using the tempera-batik method. This technique gives you rich vibrant effects as you can see in Illus. 85.

First, draw your chosen face with a soft-tip pen on construction paper of a medium or light color value. Then apply the tempera

Illus. 80. You may not think of clowns as being monsters, but there's something rather threatening about this tempera-painted jester. Is it his fixed grin? Or maybe his snake-like ruff?

Illus. 81. Here is the fearsome clown having his finishing touches applied. Notice the water-soaked paper towels in the foreground which provide a handy palette for puddles of tempera paint.

Illus. 82. A soft-tip pen is used to make the design in preparation for a tempera-batik mask.

Illus. 83. Next, tempera paint is applied. Note how the artist is careful to leave a narrow white space between the lines and the painted areas.

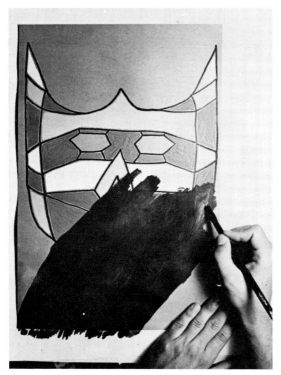

Illus. 84. When the paint is dry, an India ink and water solution is spread over the entire design.

at least 12 hours. Next, hold the paper under running water to wash away the India ink. If you wish, you can place the paper on a cookie sheet during this process to avoid tearing.

You may have to do a little finger-tip rubbing to remove some of the stubborn spots of ink, but do it carefully or you will rub away the paint as well. Allow to dry thoroughly before cutting the mask shape out of the paper. The satanic chap in Illus. 85 had his diabolical smile and eyes cut out, too.

Illus. 85. Here is the final result—old Beelzebub himself looking as pleased as Punch!

paint thickly to the design, avoiding painting over the ink lines as shown in Illus. 83. For the best results, do not add water to the paint. Also, do not paint one color over another or you will end up with a muddy look.

Allow the paint to dry thoroughly. Then prepare a mixture consisting of 3 parts India ink and 1 part water. Paint over the entire mask design with the mixture, and let dry for

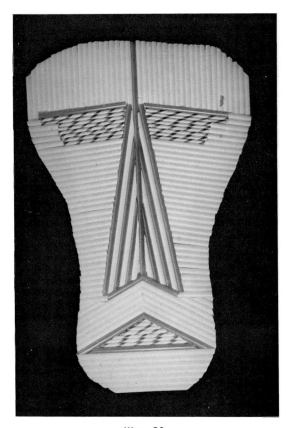

Illus. 86.

Drinking Straw Masks

Don't run—the cadaverous apparition in Illus. 86 is made of nothing more than harmless drinking straws! A variety of different kinds of straws were cut to fit this design and then pasted onto the tagboard background. Green and blue straws would lend a nice macabre touch. And perhaps yellow-and-white-striped straws for the eyes and mouth. The unhappy "you-name-it" in Illus. 87 is composed of a piece of cardboard painted with black India ink. Blue and pink straws compose his grouchy features. (He might be annoyed because he thinks Illus. 86 is worse looking than he is.)

Illus. 87.

Illus. 88.

soft, white nylon yarn glued onto a black backing. You can see here how effectively an imaginative design can transform a simple shape. Aluminum foil provides gleaming evil eyes.

The hair-raising other-worlder in Illus. 89 is completely made of pipe cleaners shaped into all kinds of kinks, bends and whorls and glued onto black-painted corrugated cardboard.

Illus. 89.

Yarn and Pipe Cleaner Masks

You can use such simple objects as yarn, string and pipe cleaners to "draw" the most unusual masks imaginable. Because of their flexibility, you can manipulate them into all kinds of exotic, one-of-a-kind creatures. If a certain "line" doesn't suit you, move it around until it achieves the proper effect.

The stark maniac in Illus. 88 is composed of

57

Tooled Copper Masks

Illus. 90. A gleaming satanic mask can be made from a sheet of very thin copper, which is easy to tool. The horns and whiskers were cut and tooled separately and then glued on.

Sheets of copper, thin enough to be tooled, provide one of the most fascinating materials for mask-making. When you are finished making one of these grotesques, your friends will think it is an example of native hand-crafting from a foreign country such as Mexico. Tooled copper masks are ideal for wall hangings. You might mount one on a piece of beautifully finished wood.

To begin, draw your design on a large sheet of paper. It is wise to keep the general outline and features as simple as possible, since the textures and patterns of tooling add a great deal of detail and variety.

When you are satisfied with your plan for the mask, tape it down on a sheet of copper foil under which you have placed a good solid pad of newspapers (Illus. 91). With a pencil or wooden modelling stick, lightly trace over the pencilled lines—just hard enough to leave an imprint of the entire design on the underlying copper.

Remove the paper and study the design to decide which shapes you would like to have raised and which recessed. Copper modelling tools are available at a very low cost, but you might use the blunt end of a spoon handle if you wish. Keeping a constant and regular pressure on the tool, move it back and forth in the areas you wish to have *recessed* (Illus. 92). When you are finished, turn the copper sheet over and your design will be reversed. Now, rub the areas that appear to be recessed on this side—they will actually be the raised areas on the "right" side of the mask. Continue this on both sides until you are pleased with the effect.

If you want to add texture as shown in Illus. 93, use the sharp point of a modelling tool or other non-metallic instrument. You can stipple, make parallel lines, checkerboard

Illus. 91. After completing your design, lay it on the copper sheet and go over it lightly with a tool to impress it on the copper.

patterns, tiny star shapes, circles, triangles or any other special effects that suit you and your ogre.

Now you are ready for antiquing (see Illus.

Illus. 92. With the blunt end of a tool, rub the parts of the design you wish recessed on one side of the copper and the high areas on the reverse side.

Illus. 93. All kinds of tooled effects can be made. Here, the mask is being stippled.

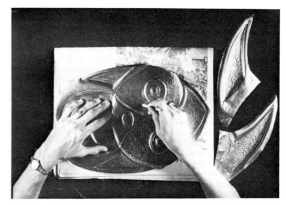

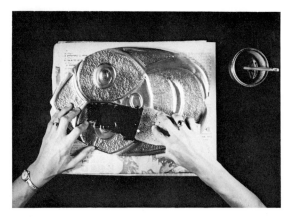

94, 95, 96). The agent, liver of sulphur (potassium sulphide), is available wherever you can buy aspirin. Dissolve the liver of sulphur in water, and then apply it to the copper with a sponge. When dry, rub the blackened copper with steel wool to bring out the highlights. To prevent the darker areas from eventually becoming grey

Illus. 95. When the liver of sulphur has dried, rub the copper with steel wool.

or chalky, you can give the mask a coat of shellac, varnish or clear lacquer.

Illus. 96. You can achieve an open, lacy effect by removing shapes from the copper with either a safety-edge razor blade or an X-Acto knife.

Illus. 97. Here is one genie no one would like to see pop out of a magic lamp! To achieve this ghoulish effect, use the crayon-resist technique described on page 50.

Illus. 98. If you prefer vampires, melted crayons are the answer.

Masks
from
Left-Overs

Illus. 99. You'd never guess what "fiendish" left-overs were used to create this enchanting fellow! See his grisly brother in color in Illus. 105.

How often do you find a spaghetti or macaroni box in your cupboard with a small quantity still left in the bottom? If you're like most people, it's pretty often. Next time, don't throw it away with a sigh. Stash all these pasta left-overs in one box and reach for it when you want to make a mask. Do

the same with cereal, rice, and eggshells, and you'll have a fine storehouse of mask-making materials.

The toothy devil in Illus. 99 would frighten Lucifer himself with his spaghetti fangs. This spine-chiller was cut from corrugated cardboard which was painted black. Pieces of cardboard were cut separately for his horns, eyebrows and nose and left uncolored. Thin spaghetti decorates his evil chin, brow, ears, eyes and cheeks, as well as his mouth. You might prefer to dye the spaghetti a bright red to symbolize his infernal nature.

When you run out of spaghetti, look what you can do with macaroni and noodles! Illus. 100 shows an awe-inspiring collection

Illus. 101. Broken eggshells colored in red and yellow provide a striking contrast with natural white shells against black felt.

Illus. 100. This unappetizing face may put you off macaroni and noodles for life, because that's what he is made of. His eyes, ears, and mouth are jammed full of alphabet noodles. Spaghettini serves to outline his features.

of different kinds of macaroni assembled into another nightmarish Prince of Darkness. All of the various parts were painted with tempera colors or sprayed with gold paint and then glued to upholstery cloth. The cloth was then pasted onto cardboard.

The timid looking ogre in Illus. 101 looks more frightened than frightening! His eggshell face is glued onto black felt on corrugated cardboard. When coloring eggshells with food coloring, dry them on wax paper.

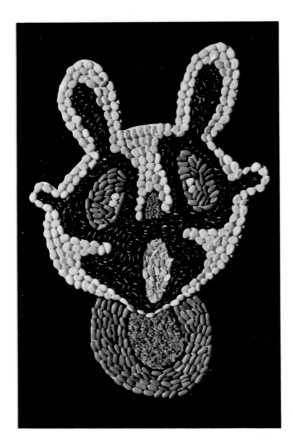

Illus. 102. This seedy character is definitely no relative of Peter Rabbit's. A piece of tagboard was used to "draw" a design on with black yarn. Elmer's glue was smeared over the entire paper before the yarn and seeds were set down on the mad bunny design.

←

Illus. 103. This vision of unloveliness probably has an aluminum heart as well as face, ears and hat. Aluminum pot-pie plates and fruit-pie containers are used to construct the entire mask.

→

Illus. 105. Two innocent materials—corrugated cardboard and spaghetti unite to conjure up a visitor from Hades. The cardboard is painted with black India ink, and Elmer's glue holds the spaghetti demon in place.

➞

◂

Illus. 104. Copper joins forces here with aluminum to create a wicked witch doctor. Sheet copper and aluminum pie plates are cut up and used as "tesserae" on a piece of black felt glued onto tagboard.

65

Clay Masks

The haunting mask in Illus. 106 is enough to make anyone's hair stand on end. The three-dimensional qualities of clay provide ample room for expression of all kinds of evil powers.

If you have a large piece of oil-cloth, lay it, canvas-side-up, on a table. On top of this, spread out a piece of cheese-cloth.

Place a large ball of clay on the cheese-cloth and set two pieces of wood, each approximately $\frac{1}{4}$-inch thick, on either side of the clay (Illus. 106). These help you roll the clay out evenly. Use a rolling pin (preferably one you will never use in the kitchen again!) to roll the clay into the shape of a flat oval.

Crumple up a double sheet of newspaper into a football shape. Lay the clay oval, with the cheese-cloth under it, over the newspaper (Illus. 107) which you should tape down onto the table top so it won't shift in the modelling process. (Be sure the cheese-cloth is in place for easy removal of the clay.)

Using your fingers, or a fork or spoon, mould the basic features of the mask as shown. You can use small pieces of clay to exaggerate and add to the features. You could make a drawing to work from, but it's often

Illus. 106. You won't need a burglar alarm if you hang this clay charmer in your window!

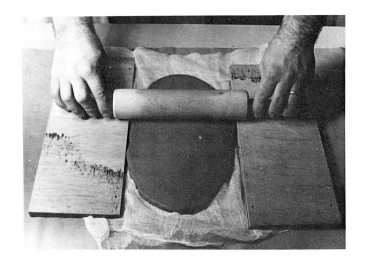

Illus. 107. Roll out your clay between two boards so it will be even on the edges.

more exciting to see the face take form without a definite plan in mind. You can punch holes on either side for insertion of a leather thong for hanging.

When the mask is leather-hard, remove it from the newspaper backing, and allow it to dry thoroughly before bisque firing. If you wish, you might glaze it before firing.

In case you cannot finish the moulding process in one sitting, store the mask in a tightly closed plastic bag so it won't dry out.

Illus. 108. Be sure you use cheese-cloth under the clay for easy removal from the newspaper form.

Illus. 109. Here's a monstrous creation that looks good enough to eat. And it is—because this fantasy is composed of dry cereals in various shapes and sizes, as well as crackers. Tempera paints highlight some of the edibles.

Illus. 110. This villainous ancient looks as though he just rose from the dead. Metal, glass, and plastic buttons completely cover his leather hide.

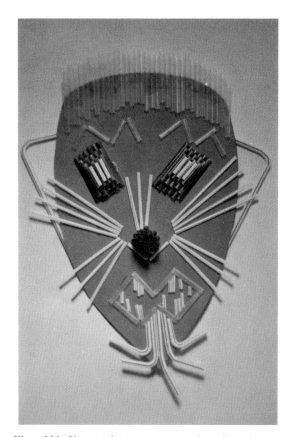

Illus. 111. No one has ever seen a banshee. Have you? This contender for the title is composed of drinking straws glued onto red construction paper.

Illus. 112. A mosaic monster mask made of broken eggshells glued onto a background of black felt. Food colorings were added before the mask was constructed.

Whatnot Masks

What are whatnot masks? It would be better to ask what they are *not!* Use everything from soup to nuts to make a whatnot monster. In Illus. 113, odds and ends of buttons of different kinds created a stunning monster effect on a crayoned design on tagboard. Black yarn outlines the absurd features which are colored in red and black crayon.

Illus. 114. This mask might be the reason that black cats have a bad name.

His weird companion in Illus. 114, who could pass for a werecat, was a simple shape made of corrugated cardboard until a multitude of colored toothpicks were glued to the black-enamelled surface.

Whatnots are everywhere—paper clips, elastic bands, staples, matches (burned), colored thumbtacks, bottle caps, small artificial flowers. The list can go on and on, but why don't you dream up as many items as *you* can, and put them to work.

Illus. 113. This mask may be ridiculous looking, but it's also frightening—a hard-to-find combination caused by an easy-to-find combination, buttons and yarn.

70

Egg Carton Masks

Although a great variety of cartons can be used in your creature constructions, egg cartons have a great deal to offer because of their interesting character. The appealing little monster mask in Illus. 116 is made entirely of egg cartons except for its construction-paper mouth.

The flat part of a cover is used here as a base. A section of six compartments is glued on to form the lower part of the mask. Part of this is cut away to allow for the downcast paper mouth. Each ear is a compartment cut in two. The eyes are formed of compartments within compartments, and the horns are each made up of

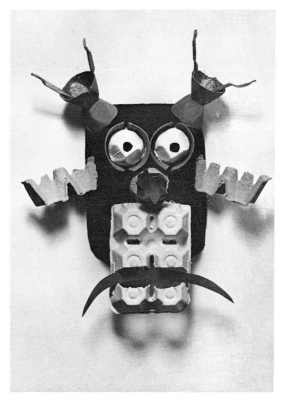

Illus. 116. This little monster appears to have sighted his prey, judging from those evil staring eyes.

Illus. 115. It's difficult to believe that this is a monster in the making!

two compartments glued bottom to bottom. The petal-shaped nose is a cut compartment, also set into another compartment. The completed egg-zotic little mask was painted in bright tempera colors—blue, yellow, white, red and orange.

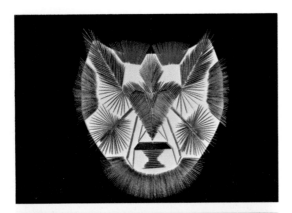

Illus. 117. A toothpick terror! These toothpicks were soaked in undiluted food colors. Wire cutters are handy for cutting toothpicks.

←

Illus. 119. Yarn usually conjures up an image of knitting by a cozy fireplace, not dancing round a hot cannibal cauldron.

Illus. 118. Is it a goblin? No doubt, since it is ugly and looks as though it is up to no good—in spite of its innocent button façade.

Illus. 120. It's hard to imagine that underneath this frightful arrangement of hair rollers, tissue paper, rug filler, pipe cleaners, and silver foil lurks an empty oatmeal carton!

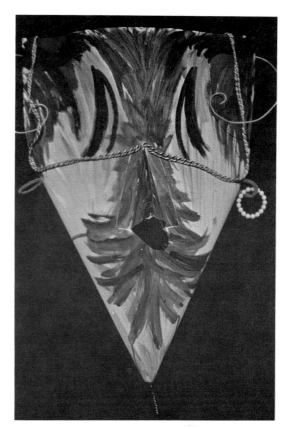

Illus. 121. You can make a fantastic phantom using nothing more than tempera paints. Here a sponge was dipped in paint and quickly whisked across a triangular piece of tagboard. You might try all kinds of dabbled effects with the sponge.

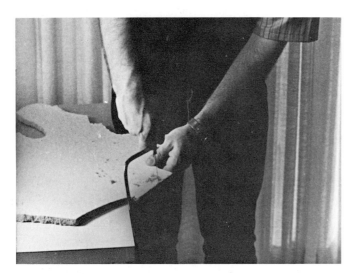

Fibreboard Wall Masks

Illus. 122. Although fibreboard is thick, it is easy to cut with a small saw.

Fibreboard is an excellent material for making wall masks—it is inexpensive, thick, and easy to saw. With it you can create spectacular three-dimensional masks. *Never wear a fibreboard mask*, unless, of course, you provide adequate ventilation. However,

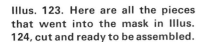

Illus. 123. Here are all the pieces that went into the mask in Illus. 124, cut and ready to be assembled.

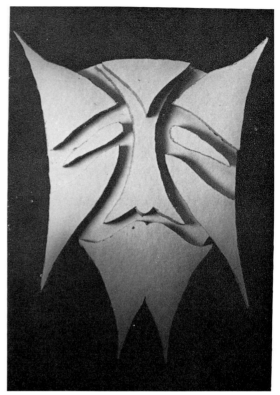

Illus. 124 and Illus. 125. These two have certainly not put their heads together to discuss the next church supper—more likely the next devil dance in the graveyard. See the chap on the right in his devilish finery on the next page.

there are so many other materials you can wear, why not just use fibreboard for decorative purposes?

The easiest way to construct a fibreboard Frankenstein such as in Illus. 124 is to sketch out a design for the parts first. Then cut them out when you are sure you have every piece you need. You can then proceed to build up a three-dimensional mask by glueing the pieces together with Elmer's glue.

Fibreboard takes tempera paint very well, so you can give some color to your creation unless you really prefer the ghastly quality shown in Illus. 124 and 125.

Illus. **126.** You can easily make a dreadful fibre-board fiend to hang up during a full moon to ward off evil doings. Fibreboard is very easy to saw (see page 74).

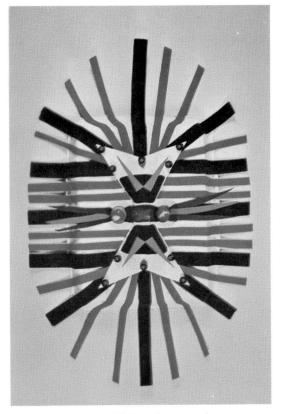

Illus. **127.** Pieces of felt radiate out from an egg-carton-lid base to form a glass-marble-eyed, octopus-like ogre. Egg cartons provide an abundance of idea material for monster creations.

Illus. 128. An unearthly wall mask is fun to make with a very earthly material—aquarium gravel. This sinister apparition was "drawn" with black cord glued on plywood. The wood was smeared with white glue, and the various colors of gravel were spread in the different areas.

Illus. 129. This heart-stopper is made of plastic foam. If you intend to wear a plastic-foam mask, make sure you have more than adequate ventilation. This mask has a very large cut-away mouth as well as eyes. See the next page on cutting plastic foam.

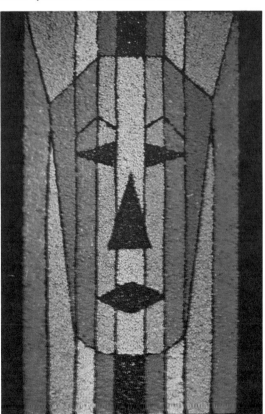

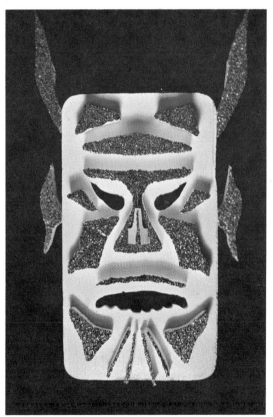

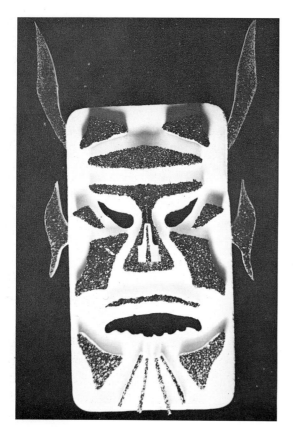

Illus. 130. Plastic foam may be weather-proof, but if you want to hang on to your friends, don't hang this forbidding zombie outdoors!

Illus. 131. Here, foam that came in a packing case is being cut with the hot-wire cutter to form the mask in illus. 130.

Plastic Foam Wall Masks

As with fibreboard, do not use plastic foam for face masks unless you provide plenty of breathing spaces. It makes an ideal base for hangings, indoors and out, and is readily available in parcels you might receive containing breakable articles. You can also find scrap pieces free of charge at a lumber-yard where it is sold for insulation in building.

You will, however, need a hot-wire cutter for mask-making with plastic foam. These are specially made for working with foam and cut it like butter, leaving a fine smooth surface. The mask in Illus. 130 has foam features glued onto a foam base. Red Christmas glitter adorns the small pieces. See him in all his gory in color on page 77.

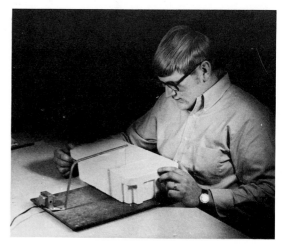

Tinfoil Bas-Relief Masks

A three-dimensional tinfoil mask can easily be constructed on a tagboard base. Although you can use a variety of materials to form the bas-relief effect, pieces of cut clothesline were used in Illus. 132. Glue the pieces of cord on the tagboard upon which you have sketched a design.

Since the effect of the tinfoil will be striking in itself, choose a simple shape such as the diamond in Illus. 132. Cut a piece of tinfoil somewhat larger than the piece of tagboard. Then crumple it up carefully and smooth it out again. Using white (Elmer's) glue, smear the areas between the pieces of clothes-

Illus. 133. Tinfoil bas-relief is used to heighten the devilish features of this chap. Black India ink lends a striking contrast with the raised areas of the shiny foil.

←

→

Illus. 134. Colored pipe cleaners can be manipulated into different shapes to form all the features of a corrugated-cardboard Mephistopheles.

Illus. 135. Make a tooled-copper Evildoer that will be worthy of hanging in the most prominent spot in your living room or den. (See page 58.)

←

→

Illus. 136. Clay allows you to create all kinds of dreadful textural effects. After you've completed a spook like this, you may be too frightened to enjoy it!

81

Illus. 137

the low areas of the foil. By leaving the raised areas shiny and unpainted, a splendid eerie effect is achieved. If you do this, make sure you lay the foil on the base with the dull side up, as the ink will cover more effectively if you do. If necessary, rub the foil lightly with steel wool before applying the ink.

Illus. 138

line, and then lay the foil on top. Very gently using your finger-tips, press the foil into the low areas of the design (Illus. 137).

If you find it too difficult to work with one piece of foil, tear or cut the foil into several pieces. The finished uneven surface will cover the telltale joined edges.

In Illus. 138, the finished mask has had an application of black India ink painted into

Illus. 139. Did you ever see a TV-dinner tray that looked like this?

Aluminum Masks

Aluminum is so abundant we take it for granted and, without thinking, toss out all of those empty pot-pie plates, TV dinner trays, and so on, never realizing how useful they can be. Easily cut with heavy shears, available in all shapes and sizes, they are ideal for monster-mask creations.

The stunning spectre in Illus. 139 has a TV-dinner-tray "face." The cut-away vegetable compartments serve as robot-like eyes, and the main course offers an ideal spot for a cut-out nose and a metallic scouring-pad moustache. Chicken-pot-pie ears and a fruit-

plate crown are held on by brass paper fasteners, as is his cream-pie-plate beard.

The deceptively innocent little fiend in Illus. 140 has a coffee-cake-container face with four pie-rim whiskers attached with brass paper fasteners. The flat parts of pie plates were cut to form the out-sized ears and pointed horns, while a piece of aluminum

Illus. 140. Aluminum pie plates and cake pans are all that you need to create bewitching creatures such as this.

Illus. 141. Dr. Jekyll and Mr. Hyde are not the only ones who lead a double life. So does this TV-dinner tray! This Mr. Hyde is attached to a piece of black-painted corrugated cardboard with brass paper fasteners, as is his fruit-pie-plate-rim "hair."

Illus. 142. Tooled aluminum containers form a vicious looking villain. You can achieve the antique effect by applying India ink, and your mask monster will be ready to perform his black arts at will.

inserted into slits in the face serves as a nose. Black yarn, glued on, emphasizes the outlandish shape of this monstrous menace.

Aluminum can also be tooled very effectively using nothing more than tongue depressors, ice-cream sticks, bone or plastic knitting needles, and so on, as tools. For directions on tooling, turn to page 58 on "Tooled Copper Masks." You can do the same with aluminum—with one important exception. When antiquing aluminum, do not use liver of sulphur as it will not oxidize. Instead, bathe the tooled aluminum with a solution of ammonia and water to remove all fingerprints. When dry, lightly rub with steel wool to dull the surface. Next, paint India ink over the tooled areas. When almost dry, wipe the mask with a cloth, removing the ink from the raised areas, but leaving it in the recessed areas. An exciting, light and dark sparkle results as you can see in the hair-raiser shown in Illus. 143.

Illus. 143. If you want to tool your aluminum creations, follow the directions for copper tooling on page 58.

Sand-Cast Masks

Illus. 144. Sand-castings create exciting, exotic masks that are intended to be hung up—not put on! This evil-eyed villain was painted with black, white, red, and brown tempera colors.

Illus. 145. Fill a tub with sand to within an inch of the top and level it off first. Then moisten with water so it will hold its shape. Here, a shallow oval is being formed with the finger-tips.

Illus. 146. A piece of tagboard, shaped into a cone, is used here to make features and decorative effects. Various objects such as stones, beads, shells, twigs, can be used to cast whatever impressions you want to make.   ⟶

Illus. 147. Place dry plaster of Paris into a bowl or basin in such a way that it forms a peak in the middle. Then slowly pour water into the basin along the edges, until it reaches the level of the peak. Mix the plaster of Paris until it has the consistency of thick cream.

Illus. 148. Use a small jar or cup to pour the plaster of Paris into the sand impression, and do it slowly so as not to disturb the delicate hills and valleys of the cast.

Illus. 149. Continue the pouring procedure until the plaster of Paris reaches the very top of the sand hollow. You must now let the plaster set until it is solid. It will not be completely dry, however.

←

Illus. 150. Loosen the plaster of Paris with a knife drawn along the edge and remove the cast mask. Then, very carefully brush away the excess sand with the finger-tips.

Illus. 151. A rinsing under a running faucet will remove the last particles of sand. The plaster of Paris casting retains the rough texture of the sand and gives the impression of being an ancient artifact.

Illus. 152. What the innocent face in Illus. 151 needs is a little color here and there to point up his repulsive character. Plaster of Paris, being absorbent, will take tempera paints beautifully. Here, an unearthly blue has been used to cover his entire face, while his spiky protrusions and mis-shapen mouth are painted aqua.

Illus. 153. His evil spirit is now completely un-
veiled by delicate touches of lilac on his cheeks
and eyes and spidery triangular forms all over
his face. An ancient oracle come to life!

Index

Acknowledgments

The author and the publishers wish to express their appreciation and indebtedness to the many people who contributed in various ways to this book: to the children of Wyoming (Michigan) Parkview School whose mask-making activities are pictured here; to the students of Grandville High School in Michigan and to their teacher, Mrs. Marcia Voet, for granting permission to photograph the masks in Illus. 22, 29, 36 and 62; to the art education students of Grand Valley State College and Michigan State University for the many ideas and examples they provided and for their assistance in photographing the art in this book; to Stella Deliyanides of Grand Rapids, Michigan, whose crayoned mask appears at the top left of this page and in Illus. 73, 74, 75, 76, 77 and 97, and whose button mask appears in Illus. 110; and finally, to the editors and publishers of *Arts and Activities* for the use of material they originally published.